Iron Man Cal

When people think about my career, I believe they think of it in a few different ways. Some people look at me as the big shortstop. At 6′4″, I was very large for a shortstop and maybe I helped change the way people viewed the position. Up until then, shortstop was pretty much thought of as a defensive position, but I proved you could be an offensive force and still play Gold Glove–level defense. Some people look at me as the guy who had all of those funny stances . . . who knows.

Obviously the thing that I am most closely associated with is The Streak. I played in 2,632 straight games, over 500 more than the player with the next closest streak—Lou Gehrig. But there was more to my career than just playing day in and day out, which was what I was supposed to do. It was my job.

My team, the Baltimore Orioles, had won the World Series in just my second season in the big leagues. That same year, 1983, I was named Most Valuable Player of the American League. It seemed like winning was all I knew in those first few years. Some players are lucky that way.

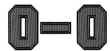

1988 was supposed to be a fun year. My brother, Bill, and I were finally starting on the same team. My father, whom I always called Senior, was the Orioles' manager. It was a dream come true for us Ripkens.

Senior had been a lifelong Oriole, a catcher in his playing days, and then a coach. When he took over as manager the season before, everyone knew he had earned the job. And when Bill was called up from the minor leagues to play second base for us at the All-Star break, it marked the first time we three were teammates. In fact, it marked the first and only time in baseball history that a father managed two sons at the same time in the big leagues.

Now, in 1988, we were together from the start of the season. It was going to be a great year.

0–1

Opening day! The best day of the season, especially for the fans. Even better, we open the season at home in Baltimore, playing the Milwaukee Brewers. The Brewers have a good team, headed by a couple of future Hall of Famers in Paul Molitor and Robin Yount. We expect to give up some runs to these guys.

We don't expect to lose 12–0. But we do.

0–2

The Orioles score their first run of the new season. I have two hits in this game, and Bill steals his first base of the season. We hold the explosive Brewers to only six hits.

Yet one of those six hits is a home run, and we lose game two by a score of 3–1. The season is a long one, though—162 games— and we are just getting started. There is still plenty of time for the Orioles to take over first place.

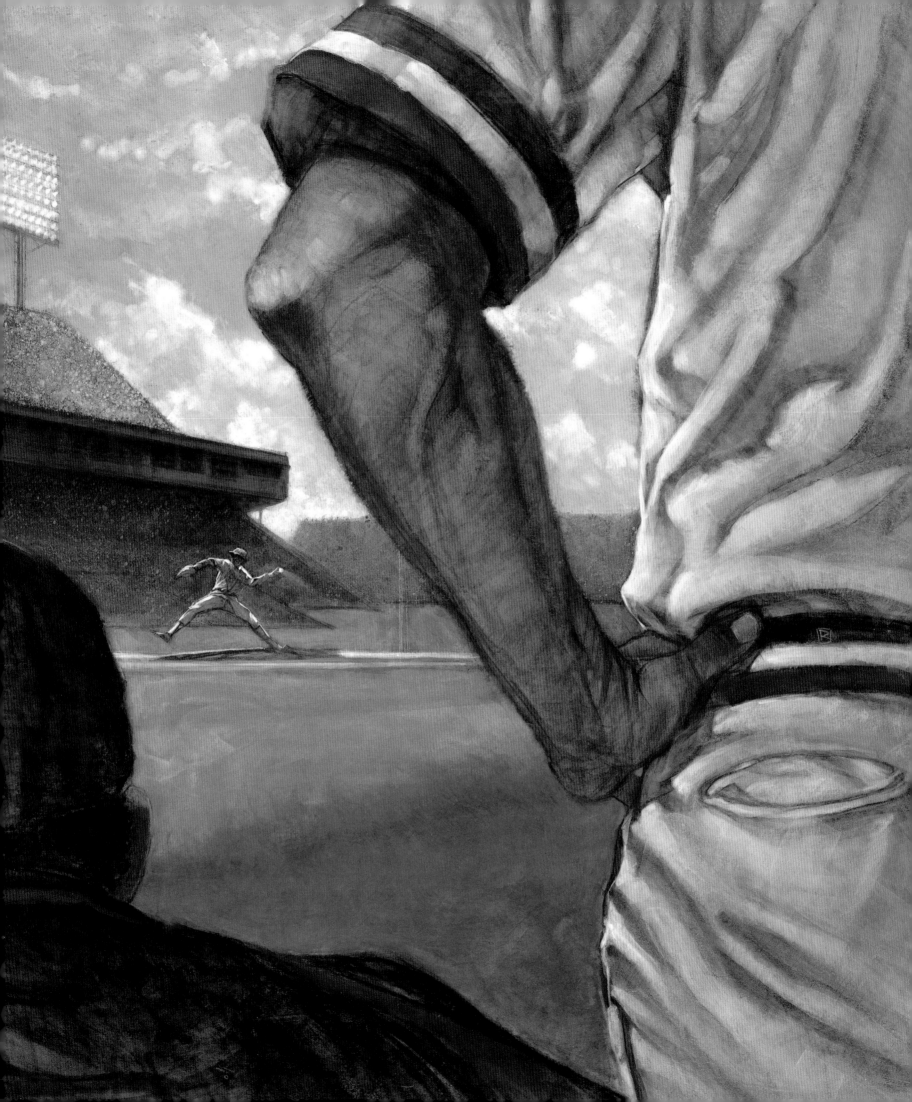

0-3

The Orioles had their turn to open a series at home. Now it is the Cleveland Indians' turn. We travel to Cleveland Stadium eager to get our first win of the season, and certain this will be the game.

It isn't. We lose, 3–0.

We all hate losing, every one of us. Especially Senior, who as manager feels most responsible. I'm not about to let my father down.

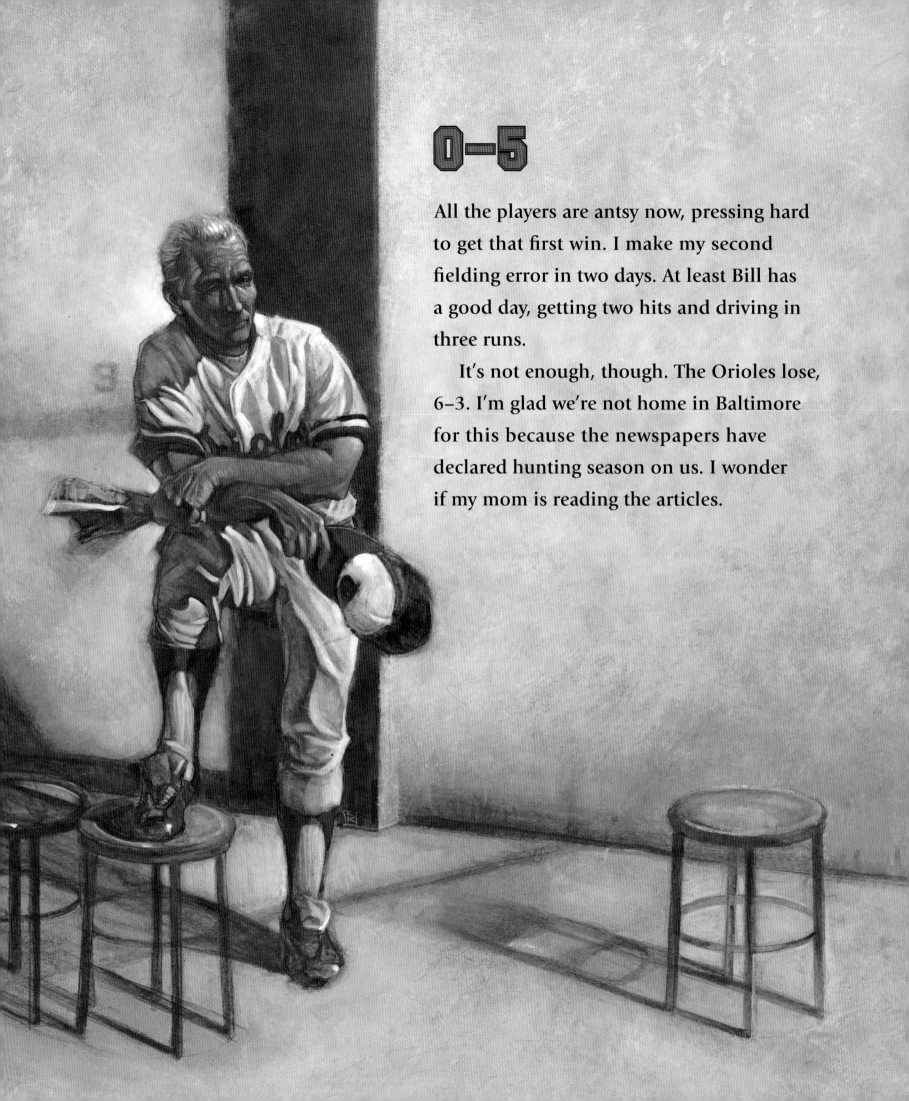

0-5

All the players are antsy now, pressing hard to get that first win. I make my second fielding error in two days. At least Bill has a good day, getting two hits and driving in three runs.

It's not enough, though. The Orioles lose, 6–3. I'm glad we're not home in Baltimore for this because the newspapers have declared hunting season on us. I wonder if my mom is reading the articles.

0-6

The worst day of the season. The Orioles lose again to the Indians, 7–2, but this loss hurts more than the others. After the game, Senior is fired as manager despite the fact that not one of these losses was his fault.

I've let my father down. We all did.

Yet it's not as though we haven't been trying. No one likes to lose, especially not me. Especially not when my father is the one who pays the price.

Now I'm angry. It is the only time in my career when I consider not being an Oriole.

0-7

A new series, back home in Baltimore against the Kansas City Royals. And a new manager, Hall of Famer Frank Robinson, a former Most Valuable Player who had been a coach on Senior's staff.

Yet the players are still stunned over this season that has turned against us so quickly. We manage to get only two hits in the game, and the Royals beat us easily, 6–1.

No one is paying much attention to my *other* streak at this point. Now all anyone can talk about is the Orioles' losing streak.

0-9

The Royals sweep the series by winning 4–3.

When I was a boy growing up in Aberdeen, Maryland, I was a sore loser. I was also a sore winner, but my parents didn't mind. They liked my competitive spirit and they encouraged me to always give it my all when playing.

It's harder to get too up or too down after a win or a loss in professional baseball. The season is long and as a player you have to keep your emotions in check.

But right about now I'd give anything for a win.

0-12

Changing managers has not cured the Orioles of our losing streak. If anyone doubts whose fault the streak really is, all they have to do is watch us play our next three-game series against the Cleveland Indians. We lose all three games and score a total of only three runs. Things are so bad for me that I don't get a single hit the entire series.

The season is only two weeks old, and already the dream has turned into a nightmare. But still, we go out there every game and give it our best.

0-18

The losing continues. Three more losses against Milwaukee and then three more against Kansas City. The entire country is now following the Orioles for all the wrong reasons. Each new loss makes national news, and the once-proud Orioles are the laughingstock of baseball.

My brother Bill becomes more famous for making the cover of *Sports Illustrated* than he ever was as a player. The photo shows him with a bat resting against his face, his head hanging down in frustration. It is how we all feel.

Can things possibly get worse?

0-20

We still haven't won a game, but when you've lost twenty straight
to open the season, you look for little victories along the way.
Today, against the Minnesota Twins, our offense comes alive, scoring
six runs on eleven hits. Bill and I have two hits apiece, and I drive
in two runs.

   The losing can't last much longer.

0-21

Twenty-one consecutive losses. The team has been on the road for ten days straight and we can't wait to get home, see our families and forget about losing.

But not yet. We have one more series to play on the road, against the Chicago White Sox. In the meantime, the Orioles have become a family of our own. When it feels like everyone is against you, it's good to have teammates.

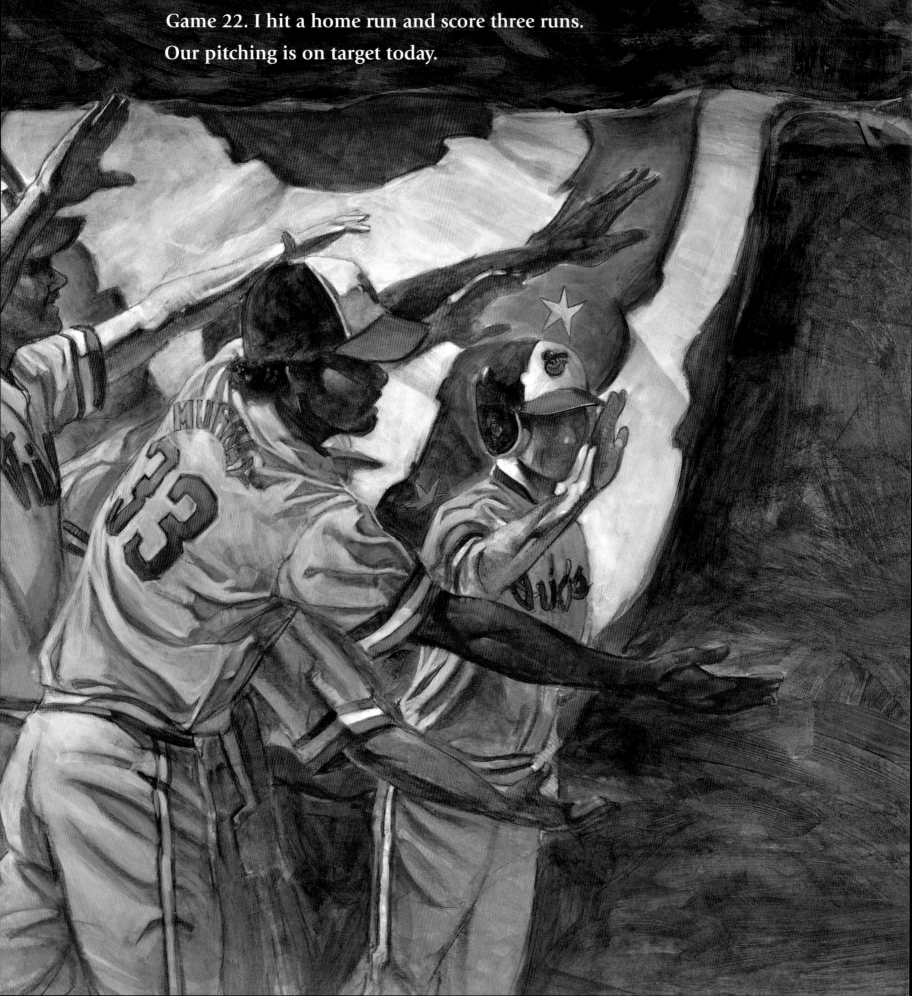

Game 22. I hit a home run and score three runs.
Our pitching is on target today.

Could it be? . . .

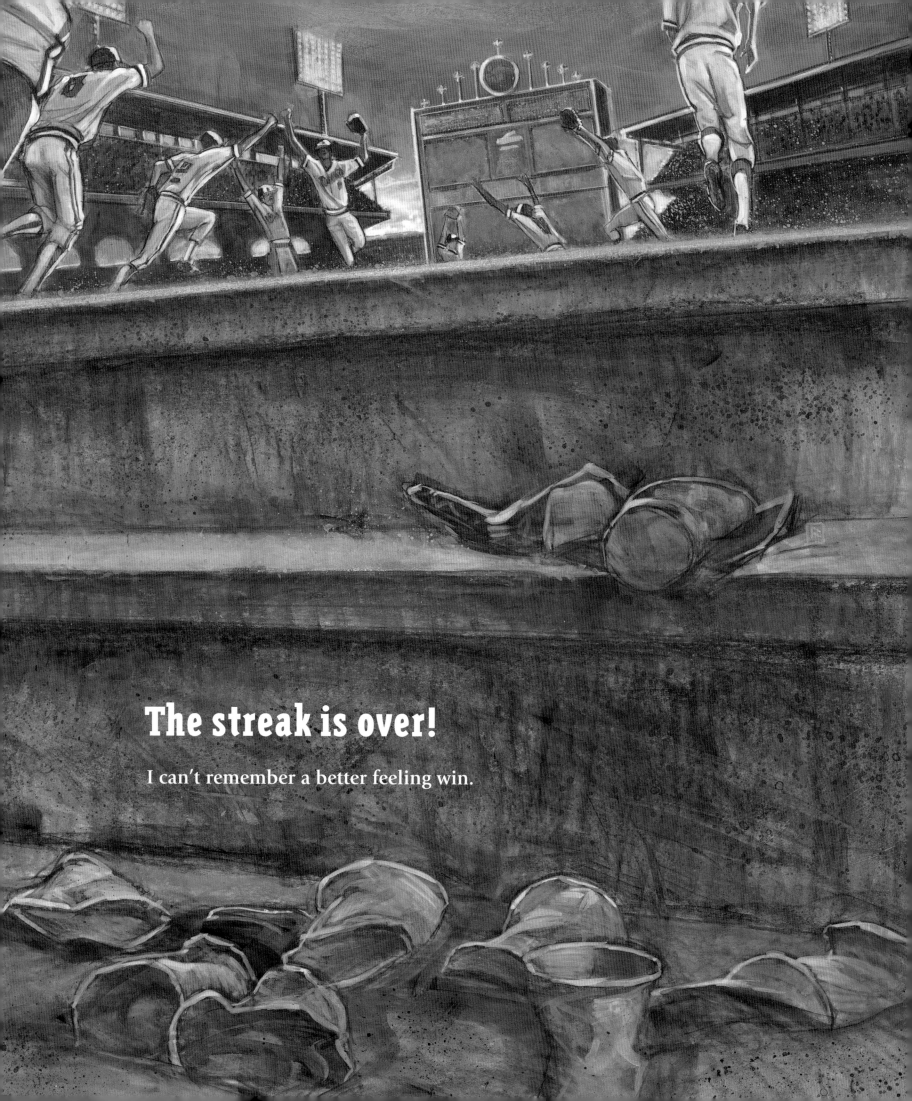

The streak is over!

I can't remember a better feeling win.

Looking back...

There is a lot I will remember about playing for the Orioles. The world championship in '83. Two MVP awards and being voted to play in nineteen All-Star Games. Over 400 home runs and 3,000 hits. And of course, the consecutive-games-played streak.

Yet the 0–21 losing streak would be the one thing I wouldn't mind forgetting, were it not for what I learned. Winning is easy on a person, but you learn more from losing. You learn to keep trying, each day a little harder than the day before. You learn how to be a better teammate, and how much you need one another to play well as a team. You even learn how to win.

The Orioles may have finished in last place in 1988, but the following year we started fresh and played together as a team the whole season. Even though we had the same team that lost twenty-one straight games the season before, we fought our way back to become winners. The 1989 season came down to the final games against the Toronto Blue Jays, with the winner taking the division title. We didn't win that series, but we fought hard—and finishing second sure beats finishing last.

To Rachel and Ryan—C.R.

To Lon and Jan, for living courageous lives—R.M.

PHILOMEL BOOKS
A division of Penguin Young Readers Group
Published by The Penguin Group
Penguin Group (USA) Inc., 375 Hudson Street, New York, NY 10014, U.S.A.
Penguin Group (Canada), 90 Eglinton Avenue East, Suite 700, Toronto, Ontario, Canada M4P 2Y3
(a division of Pearson Penguin Canada Inc.)
Penguin Books Ltd, 80 Strand, London WC2R 0RL, England.
Penguin Ireland, 25 St. Stephen's Green, Dublin 2, Ireland
(a division of Penguin Books Ltd.)
Penguin Group (Australia), 250 Camberwell Road, Camberwell, Victoria 3124, Australia
(a division of Pearson Australia Group Pty Ltd).
Penguin Books India Pvt Ltd, 11 Community Centre, Panchsheel Park, New Delhi - 110 017, India.
Penguin Group (NZ), Cnr Airborne and Rosedale Roads, Albany, Auckland 1310, New Zealand
(a division of Pearson New Zealand Ltd).
Penguin Books (South Africa) (Pty) Ltd, 24 Sturdee Avenue, Rosebank, Johannesburg 2196, South Africa.
Penguin Books Ltd, Registered Offices: 80 Strand, London WC2R 0RL, England.

Published simultaneously in Canada. Manufactured in China by South China Printing Co. Ltd.
Design by Marikka Tamura. The text was set in ITC Giovanni Bold.
The art was done in mixed media on paper.
Library of Congress Cataloging-in-Publication Data
Ripken, Cal, 1960–
The longest season : the story of the Orioles' 1988 losing streak / Cal Ripken, Jr. ; illustrated by Ron Mazellan.   p. cm.
1. Baltimore Orioles (Baseball team)—History—Juvenile literature. 2. Ripken, Cal, 1960– —Juvenile literature.
I. Mazellan, Ron, ill. II. Title.   GV875.B2R57 2007   796.357'64097526—dc22   2006008259
ISBN 978-0-399-24492-6
1 3 5 7 9 10 8 6 4 2
FIRST IMPRESSION